101

USES FOR

Silly Putty

101

USES FOR

By LINDA SUNSHINE

Illustrations by Libby Reid

A Roundtable Press Book

Andrews and McMeel
A Universal Press Syndicate Company
Kansas City • New York

Dedicated to my two favorite kids—
Adam and Alexis Dorenter—
with love from Aunt Lin.

And to Gloria Thompson from Libby.

ACKNOWLEDGMENTS

Special thanks to Brad Drexler, Edward Klagsbrun, Dennis Malloy, Donna Martin, Madeleine Morel, Lisa Shadid, Toni Simonetta, Anthony Sora, Lena Tabori, Tom Thornton, and Marilyn Vogel.

CONTENTS

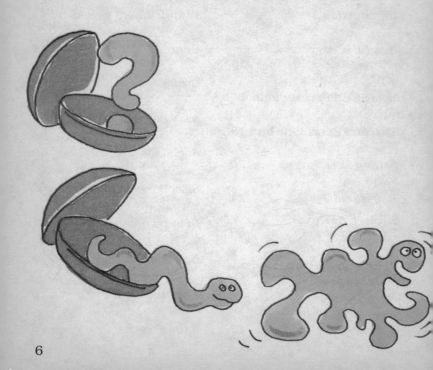

From the post-war laboratories of America's industrial complex to the aisles of K mart, SILLY PUTTY has been the toy of choice for baby-boomers and couch potatoes alike. SILLY PUTTY is the granddaddy of all the great American fads. While the average American fad has a life span of six months, SILLY PUTTY is practically middle-aged, older than Frisbee®, Barbie, and G.I. Joe. It has far outlived pet rocks and hula hoops. And, like all the great fads, no batteries are required.

SILLY PUTTY has only one moving part, and it's not a joystick.

Amazing Facts and Stats

Consider this: Since it first appeared on the market, more than 200 million SILLY PUTTY eggs have been sold. That's about 3,000 tons. How much is that?

Enough to make a giant wad the size of the Goodyear blimp!

Enough to circle the world three times—without stretching!

A recent marketing survey revealed that SILLY PUTTY is almost universally known by more than 9 out of 10 children between the ages of 5 and 12 and mothers between the ages of 18 and 40. Approximately 97 percent of all American households recognize the SILLY PUTTY name and 70 percent have purchased it. Unlike most toys, SILLY PUTTY gets repurchased. Children between the ages of 5 and 12 will normally buy or receive SILLY PUTTY three or more times!

And, how does the typical American child feel about SILLY PUTTY?

TABULAR CHART OF HOW CHILDREN FEEL ABOUT SILLY PUTTY—BY GENDER			
	Total	*Male*	*Female*
	%	%	%
AWESOME	69	74	64
Liked only THIS MUCH	15	8	24
OK, I guess	14	18	9
YUCKY	1	—	3

Conclusion

More boys use the adjective "awesome" and more girls prefer "yucky." Interestingly enough, scientists have discovered the same results in opinion polls surveying how married adults feel about sex.

Uses and Abuses

Children use SILLY PUTTY for many purposes including bouncing, stretching, lifting images off comic books, molding, and squishing shapes.

But SILLY PUTTY is also an adult toy that has found its way into the boardroom, classroom, and examining room.

Geologists use it in experiments to mimic the earth's crust.

Doctors use it in preparing patients for CAT scans as SILLY PUTTY has the specific gravity of human flesh.

Building contractors use it as a temporary leak-stopper during mock-up testing of building panels.

A Madison Avenue model uses it to remove the shine from her nose during photography sessions under hot lights.

Opticians use it to clean eyeglasses.

Zoologists at the Columbus Zoo in Ohio use it to take hand- and footprints of the gorilla population for casting replica prints.

An airline included it in their survival kit.

Professional athletes, especially baseball players, wide receivers, and tennis players, use it to build muscles and flexibility.

Business executives use it to bounce from job to job.

Lawyers use it to stretch the truth.

SILLY PUTTY even has international uses as well. It is recommended by the State Department as the one perfect gift item to take to Russia on diplomatic trips. Indeed, an unindentified White House source claimed that former President Richard Nixon was once quoted as saying, "I tried to bounce SILLY PUTTY off the Great Wall but the !@#$&! stuff wouldn't bounce straight!"

Reality Check

Yes, SILLY PUTTY is a totally useless substance, but through the years it has been proven unbelievably versatile for any number of uses. In the following pages, we reveal both the real and the not-so-real uses for SILLY PUTTY.

The essence of SILLY PUTTY, though, is that it

allows you to use your imagination and create something totally unique. It seems only appropriate, then, that a book about SILLY PUTTY would stretch the truth a little bit—so don't believe everything you read here.

In short, this book will reveal everything you always wanted to know about SILLY PUTTY . . . but were too silly to ask!

Trick a chicken

HOW Silly Putty
WAS INVENTED

Silly Putty was discovered, quite by accident, in the 1940s as scientists in the General Electric labs worked to create a synthetic rubber compound to aid the Allied effort in World War II. A Scottish chemical engineer named James Wright combined boric acid and silicone oil in a beaker. Immediately, a gooey mass formed which, when inadvertently dropped on the floor, bounced up and hit Wright in the kisser. He soon discovered that the putty could also stretch, break apart, and shatter when hit with a hammer.

GE sent tons of the weird material to engineers and college students all over the country, asking, "Can you find a use for this stuff?" The overwhelming response was, "Duh?"

No one could find a use for the putty and not one student thought about using it as a toy.

Six years later, an unemployed advertising executive named Peter Hodgson tried to sell the putty as a gift item through an ad in a book catalog. To everyone's surprise, the putty outsold every item in the catalog—except for a fifty-cent box of Crayola® crayons.

Already $12,000 in debt, Hodgson borrowed

$147 to buy a big batch of the putty from General Electric. He came up with the name SILLY PUTTY, packed it in plastic eggs, and carried dozens of samples to the annual Toy Fair in New York. A few months later, *The New Yorker* ran a short piece about SILLY PUTTY. Doubleday bookstores were one of the first retail outlets to sell SILLY PUTTY, and the stores sold so many eggs that Hodgson received 250,000 orders within three days.

When asked to describe the reason for its appeal, Hodgson replied, "You don't have to knock yourself out figuring how to use it."

When Hodgson died in 1975, he left an estate valued at $140 million dollars.

HOW Silly Putty IS MADE

Every single day, more than 12,000 eggs (or 300 pounds) of Silly Putty are manufactured at the putty plant in Pennsylvania.

Visitors to the plant must procure an ID pass, which is made of Silly Putty so that it adheres to clothing, foreheads, and noses.

The plant also manufactures other school sup-

Packing the putty

plies and visitors are warned, before entering the plant, that the combined odors of chalk dust, modeling clay, and crayon wax can cause a severe case of Kindergarten Flashback.

Production begins when the secret ingredients are mixed in a huge Cuisinart®. Then, the massive wad of putty is removed and pushed into the "Pelletizer" by a big guy named Harold. Pellets of putty fall onto an assembly line where they are packed into plastic eggs.

Last year more than 10,000 school children visited the plant. Thanks to strict safety regulations, only three kids fell into the putty vat. "Of course, they all bounced back out," adds a company spokesperson.

THE SILLY PUTTY TIME LINE

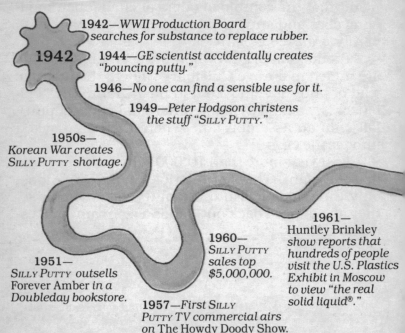

1942

1942—*WWII Production Board searches for substance to replace rubber.*

1944—*GE scientist accidentally creates "bouncing putty."*

1946—*No one can find a sensible use for it.*

1949—*Peter Hodgson christens the stuff "SILLY PUTTY."*

1950s—*Korean War creates SILLY PUTTY shortage.*

1951—*SILLY PUTTY outsells Forever Amber in a Doubleday bookstore.*

1960—*SILLY PUTTY sales top $5,000,000.*

1957—*First SILLY PUTTY TV commercial airs on The Howdy Doody Show.*

1961—*Huntley Brinkley show reports that hundreds of people visit the U.S. Plastics Exhibit in Moscow to view "the real solid liquid®."*

1966—*New Jersey man records* Silly Putty *theme song. Never published. He can't sing.*

1968—*In sterling silver eggs,* Silly Putty *flies to the moon with the Apollo 8 astronauts.*

1970—*High school boy in Kansas City gives a five-minute talk to classmates on* Silly Putty. *Gets an "A."*

1968—*John Payson honored by the New Haven Rotary Club for his contribution to American business by marketing* Silly Putty *in Europe.*

1990

1990—Silly Putty *celebrates its 40th Anniversary party, held at a swanky New York City restaurant, attended by society patrons and downtown artists. Everyone acts silly.*

SELLING SILLY PUTTY

SILLY PUTTY is more than just a cheap pick-up and, for the past four decades, it has been successfully marketed to the public. The campaign to sell the product began with the selection of a name for the bouncing putty. In March of 1950, Peter Hodgson studied fifteen different choices and finally selected SILLY PUTTY because ". . . it summed up the product perfectly." He decided to package the product in an egg, because, for breakfast that morning, his wife had served poached eggs on whole wheat. "I wanted French toast but we were out of maple syrup," Hodgson told a reporter for the *New York Times.*

Failed Advertising Campaigns

Because sales for SILLY PUTTY skyrocketed after an article appeared in *The New Yorker*, Hodgson realized the power of the media in selling his product. He advertised on radio and on the popular *Howdy Doody Show.* "Howdy was a big star at the time and his endorsement meant a lot to kids," explains Princess SummerFallWinterSpring, one of Howdy's costars on the show. "At first, Howdy was intimidated, I think, by silicone by-products. He felt that kids should play with natural substances like wood and rock. But then, one day, Howdy had a problem with his kneecaps—it was termites, if I recall correctly—but he didn't discover the problem until two minutes before air time. Quick-thinking Buffalo Bob plugged up Howdy's knees with SILLY PUTTY and, after that, the wood man freely sang its praises to the peanut gallery!"

Hodgson's television campaign was a big success and he went on to use the media in many creative ways. Because he didn't believe in using high-priced advertising agencies, some of his campaigns were, at best, rather lame. Many of his proposed advertising slogans, recently discovered in the SILLY PUTTY warehouse, never made it off the drawing board. These include:

"Fly Me! I'm SILLY PUTTY!"

"Where's the Putty?"

"SILLY PUTTY and You: Perfect Together!"
"We're the Putty Generation!"
"SILLY PUTTY . . . The Heartbeat of America!"

Marketing experts today are still studying the reasons why the campaign to market SILLY PUTTY as an adjunct to Hamburger Helper® never got off the ground.

The Competition

SILLY PUTTY is not the only putty on the market. Over the years, many other putties have tried to make it in the marketplace, but none have succeeded. For example, Patty Putty never garnered more than a 2 percent share of the market, and only last year, Stupid Putty declared itself in Chapter 11.

The reasons why other putties have not been able to capture the attention of the public are perhaps best understood by this true story from the *New Haven Register*. A few years ago, a Chicago paper ran a contest on letters from kids at camp. The winner was a letter written by a boy who was mad at his parents because they sent him a Brand X kind of putty. "I wanted SILLY PUTTY," wrote the boy, "because you get twice as much and it's more fun."

It was rumored, at the time, that Hodgson had promised the little camper a lifetime supply of SILLY PUTTY, but the allegations were never proven in court.

HOUSEHOLD USES

SILLY PUTTY is the one perfect substance for cleaning and repairing countless household items. You can use SILLY PUTTY to fix gaskets, stop leaks, seal windows, and repair faulty plumbing.

Plug up cracks or holes in your wall. Or use a giant wad of SILLY PUTTY to cover that picture window in the living room.

SILLY PUTTY works great as insulation for your attic and basement. You can soundproof the bedroom of your guitar-playing son by covering his walls with SILLY PUTTY.

Use a dab of SILLY PUTTY to stabilize wobbly tables, chair legs, or cracks in the foundation of your home.

Furnace on the fritz? During a prolonged cold snap, a SILLY PUTTY buyer in Detroit, Michigan, wrote that the pink stuff was great to have to massage and take the cold out of her fingers. It didn't prove as useful, however, in helping her defrost the freezer or start the car in winter.

SILLY PUTTY does have a valuable place in the kitchen. Use it to practice tossing a pizza crust or cookie-cutting techniques.

Everyone knows that SILLY PUTTY is a great pick-up tool for use with comic books. But, did you also know that SILLY PUTTY has other pick-up abilities? Take it along when shopping at your local grocery and use that SILLY PUTTY to pick up a carton of milk.

SILLY PUTTY is a wonder cleaning tool. Use it to remove lint and food crumbs from furniture, especially after your brother-in-law devours a box of pretzels while watching television in your den. A massive wad of SILLY PUTTY will remove your brother-in-law from the den.

Remove crumbs from your couch with SILLY PUTTY.

25

WITH Silly Putty!

Use SILLY PUTTY for decorator accessories throughout your home. You can create a SILLY PUTTY credenza or add a SILLY PUTTY baby grand piano to your living room.

Remodeling with SILLY PUTTY

Creative homeowners have done wonders to their living environments with a little bit of imagination and a lot of SILLY PUTTY. Gregory Crater, a construction worker in New South Weaver, Montana, added a second garage to his home, made completely out of SILLY PUTTY. "It was a snap," said Crater, "and I didn't need any nails. The roof gets a little soft in the rain but, what's really great is that now—when the wife backs into the garage door—she doesn't dent the Nova. And when we bought the boat, all I had to do was stretch out the back wall to make room for it."

In the home, SILLY PUTTY combines the best elements of a super cleansing agent, building material, and repair tool. "Now if it could only pay the mortgage, it would be perfect," sighs Mrs. Crater.

Important Note to Parents

SILLY PUTTY can be removed from fabrics and carpets by using rubbing isopropyl alcohol and a little bit of patience. Of course, scissors work, too.

SILLY PUTTY is great for picking up cat hair.

BEAUTY AIDS

SILLY PUTTY is a miraculous substance that can make you more beautiful, enhance your sex appeal, and save you a bundle at the cosmetics counter. In fact, SILLY PUTTY has been used in Hollywood for decades to make stars more glamorous in front of the camera. "SILLY PUTTY is an alternative to expensive plastic surgery," reports a famous Los Angeles makeup artist. "It's fast and cheap, like many of my clients."

With just a little dab of this beautifying putty you, too, can be a Movie Star For A Day. Men and women can use SILLY PUTTY to re-create:

- A Barbra Streisand profile
- Full lips like Kim Basinger
- Shirley Temple dimples
- Diana Ross hair
- Elongated legs like Julia Roberts
- A Kirk Douglas cleft chin
- A Jimmy Durante nose
- Tom Cruise teeth. And more!

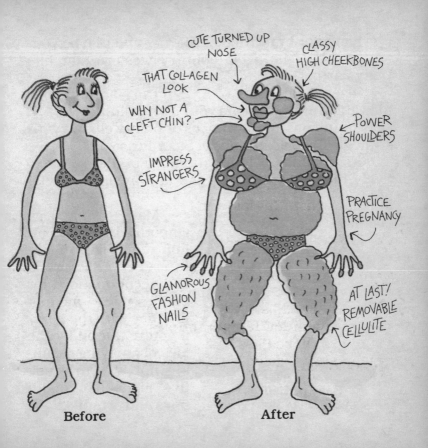

Pad your bra with SILLY PUTTY and maybe you, too, can become a big country western star like Dolly Parton.

Place small wads of SILLY PUTTY around your hips and thighs to create your own cellulite.

Round out knobby knees or pointy elbows with strategically placed globs of SILLY PUTTY.

As a makeup foundation, SILLY PUTTY effectively hides blemishes, scars, and unsightly facial hair.

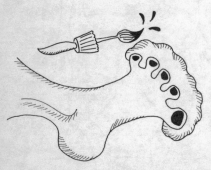

Easy pedicures with SILLY PUTTY!

Make your legs smooth as silk by coating them with SILLY PUTTY. SILLY PUTTY is also recommended for painless leg waxing. Practice with the putty if you're put off by the idea of applying steaming hot wax to sensitive areas like bikini lines and armpits.

Bored with your short hair? Attach strands of SILLY PUTTY to your head to create long, luxurious pigtails, a ponytail, or a sophisticated French knot. Or make your own dreadlocks.

Surprise your family and friends by creating fake pierced ears. A dab of SILLY PUTTY on the tip of your nose will hold a nose ring for a major fashion statement.

No woman should get dressed without SILLY PUTTY. It's perfect for removing dandruff from your black garments, which, in the 1990s, means 97 percent of your wardrobe.

Use SILLY PUTTY to mold designer shoulder pads. A giant wad on each shoulder will make you look longer and leaner and, because of the adhesive quality of the putty, you won't be embarrassed by floating figure enhancers.

SILLY PUTTY can also be molded into countless fashion accessories like big buttons, bows, belts, barrettes, hair clips, and appliques. And the putty is essential for remodeling your shoe wardrobe. Convert sneakers into high heels or flats into cowboy boots with SILLY PUTTY. Add a perky tee-strap to those old pumps. A SILLY PUTTY evening bag can be stretched into a fashion backpack if the need arises to carry home a doggie bag from the evening's dinner.

Use SILLY PUTTY to make your own luggage—a matching, putty-colored set. For that designer flair, you can make a pattern in the sides of your new luggage by carving out your initials.

The biggest fashion news this season from Seventh Avenue is polka dots and, with the aid of SILLY PUTTY, you can add dots to almost any article of clothing in your closet.

Save money on expensive eye wear by molding your own glasses from SILLY PUTTY. Create truly effective sunglasses by molding SILLY PUTTY to the lenses of your glasses. (Note: This technique is not recommended for contact lenses.)

Grooming Aids for Men

SILLY PUTTY also belongs in every man's briefcase. Attach SILLY PUTTY to your face to hide that

**Painless leg waxing with SILLY PUTTY.
No effort! No pain! No results!**

five o'clock shadow without having to shave.

Any man can simulate baldness by placing a giant wad of SILLY PUTTY on his head. Or use lots of SILLY PUTTY and be a Conehead!

Mold yourself a Tom Selleck mustache to really impress the chicks.

Embarrassed by big ears? Flatten those Dumbo look-alikes to your skull with a little dab of SILLY PUTTY.

Married men on the prowl can camouflage their wedding rings by covering the telltale jewelry with SILLY PUTTY.

Hide those embarrassing tattoos with SILLY PUTTY, especially after you've tattooed another woman's name to your forearm.

Be taller with SILLY PUTTY. Add a dab in each shoe for a remarkably effective lift to your stature.

Impress your friends by molding a Mercedes Benz insignia and attaching it to the hood of your Pinto.

The SILLY PUTTY Diet

Men and women alike can lose weight with SILLY PUTTY! Mold fake food and, instead of eating it, squish it down and mold your next course. Start with an appealing appetizer, say, angel hair pasta, and work your way to a fattening dessert like an ice cream sundae with bananas, nuts, and piles of whipped cream. Get the feel of an entire, full course dinner without consuming one calorie. (Note: Although SILLY PUTTY is a non-toxic substance, we do not recommend serving it to your family or friends or eating it yourself. Like most things that are low in cholesterol, fat, and calories, it just doesn't taste very good.)

RELIEVE STRESS
WITH SILLY PUTTY

SILLY PUTTY is utterly baffling, completely mad, and loads of fun. Many psychiatrists feel it ought to be psychoanalyzed. However, these same psychiatrists concede that, unlike people, SILLY PUTTY couldn't pay $125 per session. So why bother?

For people, SILLY PUTTY is a miracle substance for reducing tension and eliminating stress from everyday life. You can use SILLY PUTTY to do all the aggressive things you ever wanted to do—including punching, hitting, squashing, squeezing, flattening, bouncing, and throwing—all without having to worry about poking out somebody's eye.

Psychiatrists often use SILLY PUTTY in their practice, with amazing results. "It's great to use when patients are very nervous or anxious," reports Dr. Thaddeus Righthead. "As a patient plays with SILLY PUTTY, he becomes visibly calmer and calmer. It's also interesting to me, as a professional, to pay attention to the kinds of shapes my patients mold with SILLY PUTTY. You wouldn't believe how many people mold a replica of their mother and then ask me what to do with her."

Dr. Righthead also recommends SILLY PUTTY for his Group Therapy sessions. "We take a big blob of SILLY PUTTY and toss it around the room. Whoever catches the SILLY PUTTY must reveal exactly what he or she is thinking at that moment. You wouldn't believe what bizarre thoughts these people come up with. I'm amazed at what dirty minds they have!"

Quit smoking!
Reach for the SILLY PUTTY
instead of a cigarette!

Prospective patients should be warned, however, that SILLY PUTTY can be habit forming. "I've worked with people who form unusually strong bonds with their SILLY PUTTY," Dr. Righthead reveals. "One of my patients, I'll call her Molly, molded her SILLY PUTTY into a giant security blanket and named it Silly Blankie. Molly refused to leave her house without Silly Blankie, even when she had to speak before the PTA. Her 6-year-old daughter was mortified and came to me for advice. I told her that Mommy was just going through a period of intense insecurity, but I don't think the kid bought it."

Silly blankie

For such extreme cases, the good doctor offers counseling through his affiliation with the non-profit organization, SILLY PUTTY Anonymous. Members of SPA meet once a week to share their feelings, hostilities, and SILLY PUTTY sculptures. During the meetings, individuals acknowledge their addiction by standing up in front of a group of their peers and stating, "My name is _____ and I am addicted to SILLY PUTTY." Gradually, patients are weaned off of SILLY PUTTY by learning to substitute materials such as plastic wrap and cotton balls.

Of course, SILLY PUTTY has application for the lay person as well as the professional. At home, you can create a secure, private oasis for yourself by turning that spare bedroom into a comfortable padded cell.

A SILLY PUTTY straitjacket can be particularly useful on those days when PMS makes you or your spouse too irritable to live with.

SILLY PUTTY is highly recommended in helping people break their addictive habits. Yes, you can stop smoking with SILLY PUTTY. Instead of lighting up a cigarette, people are advised to reach for a wad of putty. SILLY PUTTY makes the perfect smoke-free cigarette and it can be molded into any brand—filtered, unfiltered, 100s, or lights.

WORKING OUT WITH SILLY PUTTY

You don't have to be rich to reap the benefits of a Personal Trainer. For only pennies a day, SILLY PUTTY can be molded into the perfect Personal Trainer. And, since SILLY PUTTY can't talk, it won't keep screaming at you to "go for the burn."

Flattened out, SILLY PUTTY makes a perfect exercise mat.

Yes, working out with SILLY PUTTY can be fun and rewarding if you follow these helpful suggestions.

Use SILLY PUTTY as hand weights.

Wrap putty bands around your calves for more resistance during leg lifts.

Attach SILLY PUTTY to your heels to ensure that your feet stay firmly planted on the floor during sit-ups.

Two wads of the putty, added to your sneakers, are effective shock and odor absorbers.

If you're particularly lazy, let SILLY PUTTY do all the stretching for you.

Aerobics instructors offer this advice to anyone attempting to exercise with SILLY PUTTY: Remember to breathe during exercise, and afterward, or else you'll suffocate.

SILLY PUTTY at the gym

FAMILY LIFE

At the University of Southern New Hampshire, Sociology Professor Dr. Raymond Rheinhart often compares SILLY PUTTY to certain members of the typical American family. "SILLY PUTTY is just like your obnoxious Uncle Melvin," Dr. Rheinhart tells his students. "It's totally useless—and it has been around ever since you were a kid."

He cites the longevity of SILLY PUTTY as a metaphor for parental behavior. "It's 40 and still silly, just like your dad."

When a reporter asked Dr. Rheinhart how he invented this unique perspective on family relations, the good professor referred to his own childhood. "I played with SILLY PUTTY throughout my childhood. I used to love to throw it across the room just to see what it would do. Mom went nuts retrieving my SILLY PUTTY for me. It was more fun than spitting up on the baby-sitter."

In fact, SILLY PUTTY has numerous functions in the family environment. Shrinks recommend it as a tool for family bonding. It has also been used to repair broken homes and strengthen family ties.

Young mothers have discovered that a huge wad of SILLY PUTTY makes a perfect baby carry-all. Just wrap the baby in SILLY PUTTY and the little tyke will stick to your hip like Velcro®.

Kids have found many ways to utilize the unique molding powers of SILLY PUTTY. They can create voodoo putty siblings and then torture them in many different ways. "I made a voodoo sibling doll of my stinky baby brother Matthew," claims Warren Bernsling of Duluth, Minnesota. "Then I stuck it under the dryer and it got all gooey and gloppy. It was cool!"

With the putty, kids can also make Putty Pals, sculpting replicas of their imaginary friends.

SILLY PUTTY can provide hours of family fun, as evidenced

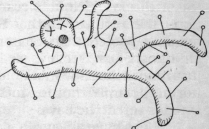

Voodoo putty doll

45

in this fan letter written by M. Burdeen, from Lubbock, Texas: "My little girl doesn't go through SILLY PUTTY as quickly as my husband and I do. We live out on an acre of land away from close neighbors and such. But we have a lot of roaches out here so one day my husband figured out a way that we could kill the cockroaches and have fun, too. We take a rubber band and load it with a wad of SILLY PUTTY. That stuff is a great roach killer! It has become a nightly sport for us. We even bought a regulation slingshot for our putty pellets! We don't buy roach spray anymore. Maybe you could have shirts made up. 'Look out Raid® and Black Flag®. It's SILLY PUTTY!'" (Note to readers: There has been no scientific verification that SILLY PUTTY works as an effective tool for insect extermination.)

Yes, SILLY PUTTY is clean (and practical) family fun, but it is also perfect for bribing kids into performing family chores. Mothers can use SILLY PUTTY in these creative ways:

"Let's have a SILLY PUTTY pull after you take out the garbage."

Family bonding with SILLY PUTTY

"You can play with SILLY PUTTY if you clean up your room."

Safety Rules for the Whole Family

When using SILLY PUTTY for family recreation, parents should remember that safety comes first and teach their children these important rules and regulations:

1) Never accept SILLY PUTTY from a stranger.
2) It's just as easy to share SILLY PUTTY with a rich man as it is with a poor man.
3) After playing with SILLY PUTTY, you can't go in the water for at least twenty minutes.
4) It's bad manners to point your SILLY PUTTY at anyone.
5) Never leave the house without a clean glob of SILLY PUTTY because you may get hit by a car and wind up in the hospital with nothing to play with.
6) Always look both ways before stretching your SILLY PUTTY.

GAMES

Silly Putty can be used for playing tennis, Ping-Pong®, soccer, squash, racquetball, kickball, volleyball, or any other sport that involves a ball that bounces and an idiot who enjoys chasing it.

Mold Silly Putty into swords for a super safe round of fencing or arrows for childproof archery.

Be the first one in your neighborhood to sponsor a Silly Putty Olympics. This exciting competition can include the following events: Discus Putty Throw, Bowling Putty, Dart Putty, Tug of Putty, Putty Toss, Miniature Putting, and the Tri-Putty-Thon.

The Silly Putty identification game is perfect for your youngster's next birthday party. One child is appointed detective and leaves the room. While he or she is out, a chunk of Silly Putty is pressed into an object in the room—a keyhole or ring, for example. Upon returning to the group, the detective has one minute to identify the Silly Putty impression or the unfortunate child must pay a huge fine.

Silly putting

Mr. Colin Carfoon of Indianapolis wrote in saying that he and his family love to fold over SILLY PUTTY to make air bubbles and then squeeze it to make strange popping sounds. The Carfoons call this activity "Outpopping Pop" and play it a lot, even though it irritates Mrs. Carfoon, who often reprimands them to "stop snapping your putty."

You can use SILLY PUTTY to mold your favorite sports figures and then cut them down to size.

For money-conscious SILLY PUTTY fans, it should be noted that the putty serves dual fad functions: You can make a pet rock of SILLY PUTTY or go hula hooping with SILLY PUTTY.

CRAFTS

Generations of families have used SILLY PUTTY for arts and crafts activities. SILLY PUTTY can be used to make coil pots, ashtrays, and sinkers for fishing. It makes a perfect foundation for floral arrangements.

Many needleworkers have tried to use strands of the putty in creating designer knitwear, but, so far, such attempts have failed. "The putty tends to stick to the needles," explains a grandmother from Ontario, Canada. "And even if you finish the garment, it always stretches out of shape."

However, SILLY PUTTY is effective in other art forms. With this versatile molding putty, you can sculpt your own version of the David (or the Donald).

Artist George Horner has used SILLY PUTTY to sculpt everything from reproductions of famous works of art to the Statue of Liberty and comical self-portraits. Some of his works have fetched up to $5,000, and a huge SILLY PUTTY canvas hangs in a place of honor in the SILLY PUTTY factory in Easton, Pennsylvania.

Artist Cherie Doyle of Minneapolis uses SILLY PUTTY in bulk to experiment with "linear laminated sculptures." She also combines imprints on SILLY PUTTY with clippings and other small objects to make documentary portraits.

These and other works of art will soon be on view at the Modern Museum of SILLY PUTTY Art, currently under construction on the fashionable Avenue of the Arts, in Los Angeles, California.

TRANSFORM YOUR PETS WITH S<small>ILLY</small> P<small>UTTY</small>

Mutant teenage turtletown

Dairydog

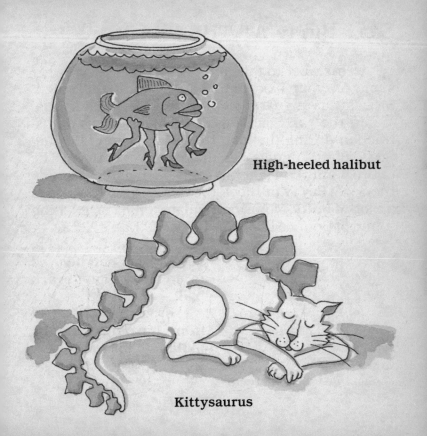

High-heeled halibut

Kittysaurus

SILLY PUTTY AT THE BEACH

Remember to take a big supply of SILLY PUTTY along on your next family vacation at the beach. SILLY PUTTY is guaranteed fun for family relaxation.

In the car, SILLY PUTTY provides hours of distraction during the long trek to the shore. Playing SILLY PUTTY games can help pass the time. The entire family can join in to play such games as Hide the SILLY PUTTY or Block the Rear View Mirror with a Blob of Putty. Moms particularly enjoy an exciting round of Bounce the SILLY PUTTY off Dad's Neck.

SILLY PUTTY sunscreen

Once at the beach, SILLY PUTTY can be used to create a giant beach ball.

Protect your feet from burning sand by molding SILLY PUTTY sandals.

Protect your eyelids from the sun with small dabs of SILLY PUTTY. In fact, SILLY PUTTY makes a perfect sunscreen for your entire body.

Pick sand off your sandwiches with SILLY PUTTY.

Of course, SILLY PUTTY can also be used to repair holes in baby Kevin's water wings or Dad's rubber ducky.

If the surf is too rough for you, build your own dock with SILLY PUTTY. Or make a SILLY PUTTY yacht and sail into the sunset with your loved ones.

Make a dream date

SOCIAL LIFE

SILLY PUTTY can be very helpful to both men and women in generating a happy and active social life. Since it was first sold in the early 1950s, SILLY PUTTY has been marketed as the toy for children "From Four to Forever" which, as many women will confirm, pretty much describes most of the men they have dated over the past ten years.

Conversely, men have used SILLY PUTTY to bounce from relationship to relationship.

Meeting

Single people in the 1990s know how difficult it is to meet prospective dates and they often turn to the Personal Ads in their local magazines and newspapers. They can use SILLY PUTTY to pick up

Make a baby

cute men and women from these personal ads and save themselves the embarrassment of making that first phone call.

When writing a personal ad, many single people use SILLY PUTTY to stretch the truth about themselves. That's why that ". . . well-built, extremely handsome, debonair millionaire" turns out to be a short, fat mailman from New Jersey.

If you still have trouble meeting someone new, use a giant glob of SILLY PUTTY to mold yourself a life-sized date. Gals can fashion themselves a major hunk with lots of putty muscles. Guys will be happy to note that, if left in the sun too long, your SILLY PUTTY date will dissolve into a very loose woman.

If your relationship with your SILLY PUTTY dream date develops into a long-term commitment and you want to experience the joys of parenthood, you can also mold yourself a SILLY PUTTY baby. A SILLY PUTTY baby is better than the real McCoy because putty babies never wet, spit up, teethe, or cry. They also will never need braces or a costly college education.

Silly Dating

On a first date, place SILLY PUTTY over your eyes and simulate the thrill of a real blind date.

SILLY PUTTY makes a clever and thoughtful alternative to candy and flowers.

SILLY PUTTY is a great little icebreaker during a lull in your conversation, although Dear Abby tells us that it is never advisable to stretch SILLY PUTTY on a first date.

You can, however, use SILLY PUTTY to relieve boredom while your date talks about her last relationship. You'll really impress her if you mold SILLY PUTTY into a likeness of your ex-wife. This tells your date, "I'm good with my hands."

SILLY PUTTY works double time in case you need to escape from a particularly geeky first date. Use the putty to make a graceful exit. Tell your date: "I'm sorry but I've got to run. I just remembered that I left my SILLY PUTTY on the radiator."

In the event that the date is a success, SILLY PUTTY can be molded into an inexpensive engagement ring.

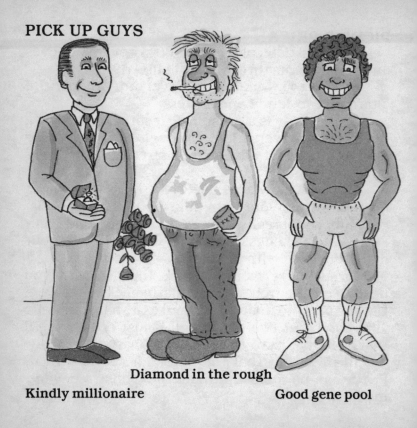

Breaking Up

We all know that breaking up is hard to do, but SILLY PUTTY can help here, too.

SILLY PUTTY can be used to mend a broken heart.

After the divorce, you can use a blob of SILLY PUTTY to cover up your spouse's face on that wedding portrait hanging in your bedroom.

Men should be advised that in most divorce hearings, the woman is usually granted custody of the family supply of SILLY PUTTY. Occasionally, though, some judges have granted weekend putty visitation rights to ex-husbands.

Repair a broken heart with SILLY PUTTY

SILLY PUTTY IN THE OFFICE

At work, SILLY PUTTY is a highly effective tool for easing tension during those nasty strategy planning meetings when everyone is shouting at each other. Pass out SILLY PUTTY and just watch everyone start bouncing off the walls.

Release tension by bouncing SILLY PUTTY off your boss the next time he makes you redraft your marketing proposal.

SILLY PUTTY serves many functions in the office environment. A small dab will alter any contract and cover up those annoying typos in your latest memo.

A large blob of SILLY PUTTY makes a conversation-stopping paperweight.

Whenever you run short of office supplies, SILLY PUTTY works double time. It can be used as a rubber band, paper clip, thumb tack, pencil holder, and packing material.

Because it can pick up images from a page of type, SILLY PUTTY functions as the most inexpensive and portable copy machine on the market.

For the finicky office worker, SILLY PUTTY cleans typewriter keys, computer keyboards, fax machines, and bathroom porcelain.

IN THE SCHOOLROOM

SILLY PUTTY is a teaching tool that can be used from nursery school to college.

Creative preschoolers use SILLY PUTTY as a substitute for the old-fashioned sandbox. "Our kids love the SILLY PUTTY box," reports Mrs. Kilgallen, who runs the Silly Day Care Center in Richmond Hills, Virginia. "Kids don't track sand all over the place and, once we finally get them into the box, they stay put."

Kindergartners have disovered that SILLY PUTTY is the perfect choice for Show and Tell. Teachers use it when reading nursery rhymes because, unlike Humpty Dumpty, it can be put back together again.

For the same reason, grade school teachers use SILLY PUTTY to teach fractions. It also makes the perfect blackboard eraser.

History teachers tell kids how Mount Rushmore was originally molded in SILLY PUTTY but Lincoln's nose kept stretching out.

Students know that SILLY PUTTY is invaluable in getting through school. Little Marjorie Helms uses SILLY PUTTY to copy her best friend's homework. "I also used SILLY PUTTY for my science fair project," reports Marjorie. "I molded a display of Imports and Exports from South America, all in SILLY PUTTY. I got an Honorable Mention!"

Her brother, Eric Helms, took the leftover putty from Marjorie's project and used it as an alternative to spitballs and paper planes, which really annoyed his substitute teacher. "I thought he was showing great creativity," said Mrs. Helms when she picked up Eric at the principal's office.

SILLY PUTTY is recommended by librarians as a quiet toy for use in the library.

And, of course, SILLY PUTTY has been used for decades by

SILLY PUTTY **study buddy**

kids all over America in getting out of a homework assignment. How often have teachers heard this old saw: "SILLY PUTTY ate my homework. Honest!"

College-bound students use SILLY PUTTY to calm their nerves during those nasty SAT tests.

At universities around the country, SILLY PUTTY is used by economics professors to explain the principle of the bouncing check.

Physics professors use it to demonstrate gradual movement of large masses of earth.

College students often use SILLY PUTTY to pick up extra credits when working toward their degree.

A few years ago, the University of Connecticut offered a SILLY PUTTY symposium as part of their unique curriculum. The course considered the philosophy, psychology, and literature of SILLY PUTTY. According to Dr. Francella Butler, UConn English professor, SILLY PUTTY "defies scientific rules by appearing to be totally what it isn't."

At Alfred University, students experimented to find out what would happen when a 100-pound ball of SILLY PUTTY (about 4,000 eggs) was hurled off the

top of a three-story building. Would it bounce, break, or splatter? The result: The ball bounced eight feet in the air, returned to earth, and shattered. When asked why the students performed this experiment, a professor of physics responded: "Well, it makes more sense than swallowing goldfish, don't you think?"

SILLY PUTTY in Literature, Poetry, and Art

Although it was "discovered" in the late 1940s, scholars have found references to SILLY PUTTY dating back to the time of Gaius Valerius Catullus (ca. 84–54 B.C.), who said, "There is nothing more silly than a silly laugh." Was he referring to the silly substance we now know as SILLY PUTTY?

Other scholars verify that Shakespeare was referring to SILLY PUTTY when he wrote these lines for Macbeth (IV,i,117): "What! Will the line stretch out to the crack of doom?"

And, certainly, in 1887, Samuel Eliot Morison was discussing SILLY PUTTY when he wrote about ". . . long stretches of pure delight."

In *Walden*, Henry David Thoreau asked: "What is man but a mass of thawing clay?" Modern scholars have noted that SILLY PUTTY would make an even more relevant metaphor for Thoreau's question.

F. Scott Fitzgerald, a notorious abuser of SILLY PUTTY, referred to his favorite toy in the epigraph to *Great Gatsby* when he wrote: "If you can bounce high, bounce for her, too/ Till she cry 'Lover, gold-hatted, high-bouncing lover,/ I must have you.'"

Poet Theodore Roethke expressed the elusive, ecstatic emotions generated by SILLY PUTTY in these lines from *The Tree, The Bird* (1964): "This last pure stretch of joy,/ The dire dimensions of the final thing."

Art critics have confirmed that *Mona Lisa* was smiling because, as Leonardo painted, Mona was squashing a ball of SILLY PUTTY in her hands.

SILLY PUTTY is often used to describe Salvadore Dali's art.

In movies, SILLY PUTTY has also been part of a long tradition. Wasn't it Bogie who quipped, "The dame is like SILLY PUTTY in my hands!"

And we end this cruise through the great art-works of the world with these prophetic lines by George Chapman: "Be free, all worthy spirits,/ And stretch yourselves, for greatness and for height."

NEW AGE SILLY PUTTY

In the New Age era, SILLY PUTTY has been proven effective for self-exploration, intuitive growth, and spiritual discovery. "It is the miracle substance for Easy Enlightenment," says guru/actress Cheryl MacWhine.

SILLY PUTTY has been used in numerous New Age disciplines including:

Astrology

In classical western astrology, the creative principle or life force is manifested in the five natural elements known to man—fire, water, earth, air, and SILLY PUTTY.

If your birthday falls between January 1 and December 31, you were born under the Astrological Sign of SILLY PUTTY. Attributes of this sign include:

Ruling Planet: Polyester
Symbol: The Chicken
Key Phrase: I stretch, therefore I am
Precious Stone: Plastic

Archetypes: Gumby, Ronald McDonald,
Mickey Mouse, Big Bird, The Tin Man,
Bambi, Sylvester Stallone
Numerology Equivalent: $1.49

Crystals

Crystals represent the magical fusion of perfect
form and earthly matter. They heal, empower, and
balance.

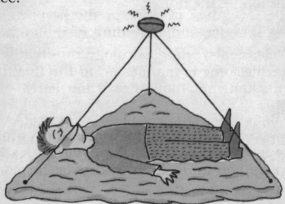

Bad vibe neutralizing putty pyramid pad

SILLY PUTTY is composed of silicone which is mostly sand and sand is mostly crystals. For this reason, SILLY PUTTY has become one of the most popular crystals known for its ability to focus energy, promote cheerfulness, lift depression, relieve stress, create warmth, heal emotional wounds, and seal car windows.

Tarot

The Tarot deck of cards predicts trends in life, creating a better understanding of the archetypal energies within each of us. These figures include The Fool, The Hermit, The High Priestess, and The SILLY PUTTY Buddy.

I Ching

Devotees of the ancient Eastern art of foretelling the future throw the I Ching with SILLY PUTTY and watch their future bounce all over the place.

Reincarnation

Through serious past-life therapy, it has been

revealed that, in its former life, SILLY PUTTY was tofu.

Psychics have predicted that, in its afterlife, SILLY PUTTY will come back as a Goodyear tire.

Karma

The adhesive qualities of SILLY PUTTY make it an effective product for cleaning your psychic aura. SILLY PUTTY can instantly remove black spots from your soul and polish a dingy aura. It will also erase negative vibrations.

Because SILLY PUTTY is available in fluorescent shades of magenta, yellow, blue, and green, it can also be used to colorize your auric field.

Predestination

According to the teachings of the Koran, you are destined to spend at least one-eighth of your earthly life playing with SILLY PUTTY.

Imagination

"I put SILLY PUTTY under my pillow at night and, while I slept, it stretched my imagination," wrote H.D. Thoreau.

Palmistry

If your personal palm reader lives in another state, you can make an imprint of your hand with SILLY PUTTY and send it via Federal Express for a convenient consultation.

Mind Control

SILLY PUTTY can be used as a medium for channeling psychic energy. Meditations on a wad of SILLY PUTTY have been known to harness self-understanding, increase psychic vibrations, and locate parking spaces in major cities across the United States.

Your Inner Voyage

Take SILLY PUTTY along on your next inner voyage. Use it to pad your self-esteem and pick up feedback. Expand your psychic skills by utilizing SILLY PUTTY for grounding your energy and stilling your mind. Build your own personal pyramid with SILLY PUTTY and impress your psychic pals!

THE FUTURE

In the spring of 1990, SILLY PUTTY marked its 40th Anniversary with the introduction of fluorescent colors. Now available in blue, green, yellow, and magenta, SILLY PUTTY has a whole new look for future generations of stretchers, bouncers, and molders.

What's the next step for SILLY PUTTY? In the near future, a glow-in-the-dark SILLY PUTTY will be marketed to the general public. This glowing SILLY PUTTY will be perfect for moonlight walks and after-bedtime putty games.

Repair the Exxon Valdez

Other plans for SILLY PUTTY include the advent of the SILLY PUTTY Buddy, The Wheel of SILLY PUTTY Fortune, and SILLY PUTTY Jeopardy. A major television company is currently developing a new Sunday evening show, tentatively entitled *America's Funniest Home SILLY PUTTY Projects.*

As we approach the 21st century, SILLY PUTTY is becoming a product of governmental importance. A Congressional subcommittee is studying plans for the application of SILLY PUTTY in helping to solve world problems. "We believe that SILLY PUTTY can aid in saving the planet," reports Senator Gerard Montlebaum, a Republican from the Southwest. "We're going to clean up the environment with the help of this bouncing putty. We can use it to pick up garbage forever."

Several bills are pending before Congress which would fund research and development in this exciting venture. Proposed legislation calls for massive production of SILLY PUTTY to help solve these problems:

> Rebuild the Berlin Wall.
> Plug up the Exxon Valdez.
> Put a mole on the Statue of Liberty.
> Repair the ozone layer.

Fix potholes in New York City.

Blanket the rain forests of Brazil.

And, yes, SILLY PUTTY is still an important part of our space program. At a recent press conference, President Bush announced his hopes that, by the year 2000, America would put SILLY PUTTY on Mars.

A FINAL WORD

Which came first? The chicken, the egg, or the SILLY PUTTY?

Tell us what you think. And let us know if you have any other uses for SILLY PUTTY.

Send us your ideas and maybe we'll use them in our next book, *101 More Uses for SILLY PUTTY*.

Write to: Roundtable Press, Inc., 80 East 11th Street, New York, NY 10003. Attention: Silly Editor.